Freshly unearthed

GHOSTLY TALES OF WESSEX

for my brother-in-law Jim Maitland
the 'happy farmer'

Patricia M Wilnecker

1995

By the same author:

non-fiction
High Street Murders 1598
Published by Poole Museum Service
A History of Upper Parkstone (beginning to 1939)
Upper Parkstone in the Second World War
More Recollections of Old Upper Parkstone
Bounty, the tale of a dog
Wessex Walkies for you and your dog
More Wessex Walkies for you and your dog
Published by Patricia M Wilnecker

fiction
The Bountifull Gyfte
Published by Patricia M Wilnecker

First published in 1995 by Patricia M Wilnecker
73 Gwynne Road
Parkstone
Poole
Dorset
BH12 2AR

© P M Wilnecker 1995

British Library Cataloguing in Publication Data
A catalogue record for this book is available from the British Library

All Rights Reserved
ISBN 0 9513971 7 6

Made and printed in Great Britain by The Local History Press,
3 Devonshire Promenade, Lenton, Nottingham NG7 2DS

Contents

		Page
1	Do ghosts exist?	5
2	Coincidences?	6
3	The South Newton Doppelganger, and other strange happenings	8
4	The Ghostly Nun in Bournemouth Gardens	11
5	Victorian Cottages ancestral ghosts, Dunford Road, Parkstone	11
6	Awareness of death, Runton Road, Parkstone	14
7	The 'Visitor', Yarrells Lane, Upton, near Poole	14
8	The many ghosts of Lytchett Matravers	15
9	The Face at the Window, Westbourne	18
10	The Caring Nun, Hamilton Road Orphanage, Boscombe	19
11	The ghost that scared the Bournemouth Plumber	19
12	New Street, Poole, The Footsteps on the Stairs	20
13	Worth Matravers' Benevolent Vicar	21
14	Hamworthy's ghosts	21
15	Amesbury - the Conscientious Pharmacist	22
16	The Strange Man of Marler House, Westbourne	22
17	Royal Oak, Bere Regis	23
18	Pudding and Pye Inn, Wimborne	23
19	Wattles Hotel, Hythe	24
20	Cornwall Hotel, Dorchester	24
21	True Lover's Knot, Tarrant Keynston	26
22	The phantoms of Smedmore House	26
23	The ghosts of Athelhampton	27

Contents continued

		Page
24	Lord Digby's Servant's apparition	28
25	Weird happenings at Rockbourne Roman Villa	29
26	The Church in the Rings, Knowlton	31
27	The Voices of Tilly Whim Caves	32
28	The Man on the Bicycle, Longham	32
29	'Annie' of Riverside Mews, Mill Lane, Wimborne	33
30	The Gypsy's Phantom Devil Horse	34
31	The Alder Hills Smugglers	35
32	Bygone Children's Voices of the Old Dorset School	35
33	The Man Who Met Himself coming back!	35
34	The Vanishing Boy, near Sidmouth	36
35	The phantom of 'Sally in the Wood', Monkton Farleigh	37
36	Poole High Street Murders, 1598	37
37	The Market Street hauntings, Poole	40
38	The Boy in White, Coy Pond's ghost, Branksome	43
39	The Strange Spoon	43

Do ghosts exist?

*'When I was walking on the stair
I met a man who wasn't there
He wasn't there again today
Oh! how I wish he'd go away.'*

Do I believe in ghosts? To be truthful, I've never actually seen one although all the people I interviewed or who wrote to me were convinced that they had, and dogs in particular can certainly sense things of which we are unaware.

I first came to hear of this via a musicologist who used to be a fellow 'digger' at Rockbourne Roman Villa near Fordingbridge in the 1950s/60s (but more of that location later!).

She and her husband lived in Ringwood at the time and in the evenings used to take their Golden Retriever for walks near the Fish Inn. There is an old stone-arched bridge nearby, now superseded by the fast dual carriageway. Although there was nothing visible on the bridge the dog's hackles rose every time they crossed it. He would growl uneasily then with great reluctance squeeze himself between 'something' and the parapet. On reaching the other side he was his normal self, trotting along happily for his evening walk.

Now I have my own dog Bounty, a Parson Jack Russell terrier, I find he too has perceptions which I have not. It was in Wareham Forest that I first became aware of it and I found it quite unnerving. His tail drooped and he skulked along, glancing over his shoulder every so often at... nothing visible to human eyes! Once we had passed a particular spot his tail rose and he resumed unconcernedly sniffing around for rabbits and squirrels.

Badbury Rings, with its long history of occupation by the Durotriges tribes then the Roman Legions, is another place where he 'sees' things. At the crest of the Roman road that heads towards Witchampton his behaviour is sometimes the same — but not every time. Perhaps there must be certain atmospheric conditions?

Bottlebush Down Roman road near Cranborne and Heron Drove near Badbury Rings are more of his 'uncomfortable' spots and again at nearby Sweetbriar Drove. I have been accompanied by friends who can confirm this strange behaviour and also that there was no obviously — to humans — apparent reason for it.

Often I have thought that with the right conditions and if our minds are tuned to the correct wavelength maybe we too could pick up events which through repeated use or enough emotional stress have left an imprint behind them. Perhaps, in future years this will be explained and we will be able to tune in to the past. After all, what would people have thought a couple of centuries ago if they had suddenly seen television? Given the right transmitters and receivers we suddenly have 'visions', apparently from thin air!

I have always lived in the same house. I was even born there. My sister married first, then my brother but I stayed at home with mother until she died at the age of 89. Sometimes I drop off to sleep in my armchair and, on waking, I am very much aware of her sitting opposite me in her rocking chair but when I open my eyes there is no-one there. This could simply be that she HAD been for so many years that my subconscious expected her to be there. Or maybe she left an impression on the atmosphere and my mind, being in the half sleeping, half waking state tuned in to her presence?

Sometimes when I am sitting by my fireside I get the distinct aroma of tobacco smoke. No-one smokes in my house nowadays but father, who died in 1938, smoked a pipe. The bungalow was built for my parents and certainly there has been no other dwelling on the site since tobacco was brought to England so perhaps father is still keeping a kindly eye on the place, too?

I like to think if my spirit roams it will choose Luscombe Valley, near Evening Hill, Poole. I walk there so often with my dog Bounty that I am sure both of us are leaving happy impressions in the air. My investigations seem to confirm spirits do not have to be unhappy. It is a peaceful place to visit and I hope Bounty's spirit will be there alongside me. Unlike most other animals, dogs and cats dream so I am sure they have souls too.

One ghost which I was told about and I would be happy to be haunted by is that of a small dog. So great was his love for his mistress that even after death he was reluctant to leave her, and appears from time to time in her Dorset home. Sometimes she only hears him and on other occasions she sees his little figure appearing round a door or sitting in his favourite chair. A friendly apparition!

***

The stories that follow are in the main previously unpublished ones and were told to me when researching my historical books or in response to my requests for ghostly experiences in the local press. I share them with you in the hope that reading them will entertain you — and perhaps you will ponder......

Coincidences

Back in the 1970s/1980s I used to belong to a small group of people who transcribed documents from the Poole archives into 'readable' English. My chief interest was the Tudor period and it was during these sessions I came across the papers relating to the High Street Murders. Much of the work was mundane, day to day records such as 'goods brought into the town', 'summonses for rubbish left lying in the street' and so on, but in these everyday events life of the period became very real to me.

Something which at first seemed amazing but as it happened so often soon ceased to be so, was the 'coincidence factor'. We would be talking about a person from the period and behold! the next document in the pile would mention him! Or we would refer to H P Smith's excellent *History of Poole* for something and find on the printed page the very document on which we were working. Time and again this happened and we often used to say jokingly, 'Someone up there is helping us with our research'. But perhaps they really were...?

I found the same thing again when researching my historical novel, *The Bountifull Gyfte*. *High Street Murders 1598* had been very successful and the then curator of Poole Museums, Graham Smith, asked if there was anything similar in the archives which would make another little book. I immediately thought of the case of Walter Meryatt and William Drake, two Elizabethan mariners of the *Bountifull Gyfte* of Poole who had been fired on by the gunners of Brownsea Castle in 1598. This HAD appeared briefly in history books but we had the actual eye-witness accounts in the archives so I wrote it up in a similar manner as before.

Time went on and I waited for publication — but nothing happened. I reminded Graham from time to time but it seems there wasn't the money available then to print another book and it 'fell by the wayside'.

Meanwhile, I had been reading ancient books on Purbeck, Corfe, Poole and Brownsea and kept finding more and more connections with the *Bountifull Gyfte* story. Realising it could be expanded and even made into an historical novel based on what really happened I went ahead and wrote it.

Again I met with the coincidences — it was as though the story WANTED to be told. One thing led to another and confirmed my researches.

I went to the County Records Office at Dorchester, wanting to find the names of the inhabitants of Corfe Castle in that period. There I found a map, drawn and coloured by Ralph Treswell, of the exact date I wanted, giving houses, field names and their owners. I then travelled to Purbeck and found I was walking where my characters had walked. 'Haycroft' had become 'Haycraft Lane'. I drove towards Studland and there was still a place called 'Woodhouse', where Francis Hawley, steward of Corfe Castle had lived. I walked down the track to Afflington Manor Farm and there the kind wife of the owner showed me the Elizabethan part, which was still lived in. The yard where Hawley kept his falcons was still there and I too trod the paving stones where he had walked. I was shown an uneven field which was all that remained of the hamlet and church of Afflington which I hadn't known existed.

Back again to the County Record Office, this time for information on the pirates of Studland. I came across names I knew from Poole Archives and then, in the middle of Customs Records I found a moving little poem written by one of the Recorders which I HAD to use in my story,

'Look where the tree doth fall
Lo - there it lies.
O happie fall, that to the Lord doth rise'

I wanted to visit Brownsea Castle as it featured strongly in the book so contacted the owners, explaining what I required. They generously sent a boat across for me and took me to the Tudor cellars which are all that is left of Henry VIII's castle below the Victorian one we see today. Here I was in the footsteps of the wicked Partridge brothers! The scour marks in the floor left by their cannon were still visible and through the gunports the same view of the harbour entrance where the unfortunate captain of the *Bountifull Gyfte* had waved his hat in the air, crying 'Hoist the main topsail' before he was gunned down.

Finally, I must relate a really strange happening. One evening about an hour before sunset I was driving from Worth Matravers to Kingston on the high road where there is a superb view across the common to Corfe Castle in the valley below. To my amazement the castle appeared to be intact, not the ruins we see today. I drew to the side of the road, climbed out of the car and stood entranced. I thought perhaps a film company had used fibre glass to reconstruct the walls for some epic, as a TV company had done for nearby Tyneham some years ago.

It made me happy to have seen it like that, complete, as it appeared in my book — my only regret being that my camera was at home. I drove down the hill from Kingston and into Corfe village. A shiver passed over my body as the castle came in sight — it was once again in ruins with absolutely no sign of a film company!

Had the castle really reappeared in its former glory, or was it a trick of the light? It certainly fooled me if it was, but nevertheless I felt very privileged to have seen it.

Are the spirits of long-dead people still captured in the past, or can they escape and influence us today? Be that as it may, I feel their stories certainly helped me write a successful and popular novel!

The South Newton doppelganger and other strange happenings

Mrs Pamela Johnson of Moordown, Bournemouth had several strange tales to tell. The first occurred when she was twelve years old and living at Newton Villa in the village of South Newton, near Wilton. It was a very old house she told me, with thick walls and a bread oven built into one in the kitchen.

Every evening her mother, Mrs Cook, would turn down the beds and draw the curtains then sometimes play cards with her daughters in the dining room. Pamela told me that one of her sisters, Bunty, used to give herself 'airs and graces' and flaunted herself in a distinctive black cape, headscarf and skirt which with her blonde hair made her look rather fetching.

On this particular day mother was upstairs turning down the beds as usual when her daughters heard her cry in horror, 'It's awful! I've just seen Bunty fall out of the window!' It was a large, old-fashioned sash window with a wide flower border below.

'I'm too scared to look!' cried their mother in dismay.

The girls looked at each other incredulously — Bunty was sitting WITH them playing cards!

A few weeks later their mother was busy baking cakes and not wanting to stop, called to the girls, 'Pam, run up and see to the curtains please.'

Pamela obediently ran up the stairs but as she reached the fatal window — there was Bunty in her black cloak, disappearing through it once more!

'Sheila!' called Pamela to her other sister, 'it's happened again!'

'Take more water with it!' was the unsympathetic reply. 'She's down here with me, reading a book!'

(Incidentally Bunty never DID fall through the window — so why did she appear to do so ....?)

***

Two months later, Pamela was sitting up in bed in a rather low-cut nightdress rubbing cream into her hands to soften them.

Suddenly what she described as a 'superbly handsome "Being" in uniform' appeared at the foot of her bed. 'He was absolutely DIVINE!' (she told me), and she ducked under the bedclothes, too embarrassed at being discovered in her revealing nightie to wonder where he had come from. When she peeped out again, silently (and to her intense disappointment!) the 'vision' had vanished.

Two weeks later, Pamela heard rapping on the headboard of her bed followed by the sound of footsteps in heavy army boots walking across the room and through Bunty's door. She shone her torch..... but no-one was there.

Bunty, thinking she was fooling around called, 'Don't wake me up, I want to go to sleep and I know you are hiding under my bed and shaking it!' The footsteps returned and something tapped on the bedhead again.

Pamela told Bunty and they checked to see if their other sisters were in their own rooms — and they were!

Every so often after that, Pamela felt something under her bed which would shake her up and down as though she was on a trampoline!

Knitting needles and other articles would keep disappearing until at last it all became too upsetting and their mother and father sold the house. They heard later from a friend that the hauntings continued after they left and the house had changed hands three times.

When Pamela was three years old, her mother told her about her grandpa, Reverend A E Norman of Avalon, Broadchalke. His wife died when she was only 21 but he lived to a ripe old age. At last he too became ill and suffered a stroke which meant he had to be fed intravenously and the only way he could communicate was with his eyes.

Then one day, he suddenly sat up in bed, waved his hands in the air with a look of rapture on his face and cried, 'Effie darling, I'm just coming!' and died.

***

Pamela is now a grandmother but peculiar things are still happening, and she assured me the story which follows is not exaggerated in any way.

Three or four years ago when she moved to Moordown her son-in-law came to say goodbye as he was emigrating to Australia. She was very sad to see him go as he was more of a son to her, even though his marriage had broken down.

'Please DO come back again — we NEED you' she told him.

Holding her face in his hands he looked deep into her eyes, saying 'I PROMISE you Pam, I WILL return.'

***

A couple of years later her eldest grandson Anton called. He was buying a house in Milton Keynes and was about to drive there with some of his belongings.

'Go in with grandad' Pamela told him, 'and I'll make some coffee.'

Leaving the two men downstairs she quickly went up to the toilet, not bothering to close the door behind her as the front door was on a chain and she could hear the only other two occupants of the house chatting below.

To her surprise, the chained front door suddenly opened and she heard quick footsteps climb the stairs. The men were still deep in conversation below and later told her they had heard nothing.

Footsteps passed the open bathroom door — but no-one appeared! Her two spare bedrooms were locked as she was 'between students' and the rooms were prepared ready for the next consignment. Undeterred, the footsteps entered the two locked bedrooms as though searching for someone, then the unlocked one opposite the bathroom — and didn't come out again.

Pamela felt an icy chill, sure that some ill had befallen her son-in-law, as she believed he was desperately unhappy in Australia. Slowly, she went downstairs to her husband and grandson. Anton looked up as she entered the room. 'Are you all right, gran?' he asked.

***

Next day, the police called to bring her some bad news — her beloved son-in-law had died in Australia. Had he fulfilled his words — 'I PROMISE you Pam, I WILL return?' She believes so.

The ghostly nun in Bournemouth Gardens

Mrs Bedford, a lovely eighty year old Irish lady told me about a supernatural experience she had one morning many years ago in Bournemouth Gardens.

She was on her way to work near Bournemouth Pier and was crossing the Gardens from the direction of the Aviaries. A flight of steps led down to what used to be known as 'Invalids Walk' and as she approached she saw a shadowy figure in a black, hooded cloak with a nun's cowl leaning on a balustrade. Upon reaching the figure it half-turned towards her. 'It had a wild, fierce expression — but it was not a human face' she told me. 'I felt very afraid, and turned and ran.'

Mrs Bedford said she understood there used to be a convent belonging to a strict order nearby which nursed TB patients. There was a story that a nun had misbehaved and been locked away as punishment. Was this her apparition, I wonder?

On another occasion the same Irish lady and her husband were walking home from a party around one o'clock in the morning. She assured me neither of them had been drinking, but as they approached number 28 Poole Road, Bournemouth they saw what at first they took to be a policeman standing by the gate. They noticed his very shiny boots, then looked at his face — but it wasn't there — he was headless!

This apparition had also been seen by several bus drivers, when buses still ran at that hour. The phantom was believed to be a French soldier who had been beheaded for some misdemeanour, and not a policeman — but what was he doing in Poole Road? It remains a mystery. A very strange affair!

Victorian cottages ancestral ghosts, Dunford Road, Parkstone

The following incidents were related to me by a lady who has lived in one of the cottages for most of her life.

One day, she was upstairs with her son, who was about three years old at the time, making the beds while he played with his toys. When the job was done she came downstairs, followed shortly afterwards by the boy who asked, 'Who was the lady sitting on your bed, mum?'

'There wasn't a lady, my love,' she told him.

'Yes there was!' he insisted and described a little lady in a long skirt with her hair in a 'funny thing' on top of her head. To his mother's amazement he

Dunford Road, Parkstone, scene of the friendly 'family' hauntings.

had perfectly described her grandmother who always wore her long hair in a bun.

The old lady had come to live in the house when she was married as the house had been built around 1900 for her and her husband. There was no photo of her anywhere, so the boy could not have picked up the description from there. My informant's grandmother and parents all shared the same house and she was brought up there.

Another strange thing which happened over and over again was a feeling she had of someone entering the room and sitting down. They owned a chair with a leather seat in those days and it made a distinctive creaking sound when sat upon. She had the impression it was the spirit of her grandfather as there was a really strong smell of beer, so strong you could almost taste it! There was also a smell of tobacco at times although no-one was smoking.

Her husband was sceptical about all this. He worked for the Post Office and slept in the daytime when he was 'on nights', but was disturbed by footsteps in the bedroom.

'I wish you would stop walking around the room when I am trying to get some sleep' he told his wife — but she had been shopping in Parkstone and there was no-one else in the house! This happened several times but he could never believe it wasn't her!

***

The same lady told me that gloves, letters and other objects would appear in different places from where they had been left, as though someone — or something — had been looking at them.

***

When her daughter moved to another house nearby which had been unoccupied for two years there was a really strong smell of violets in the house, so strong that her mother could smell it on her clothes when her daughter came to visit her. The smell grew stronger and stronger and it is believed that there was a violet farm on the site many years ago. A ghostly, lingering perfume — a pleasant haunting.....

***

The lady's son-in-law told her that they were inspecting the house prior to purchase when he saw a man standing in the hallway, wearing a seaman's dark jacket and a peaked sailor's cap. My informant said this was a perfect description of her great uncle who had also lived in that house at the turn of the century.

***

When the children were small, the baby used to lie in her pram in the garden laughing, chuckling and stretching out her arms to someone..... but there was no-one there. This often happened.

***

The lady's daughter used to say that she could hear scissors snip, snip, snipping away. They could find no reason for this until her mother mentioned it to an uncle who told her that her grandfather used to cut hair in what was then the front room of the house.

***

The lady told me her grandfather was one of a family of 13 who came from Brownsea Island and used to work for the Van Raalte's. Their employers had a Scottish housekeeper who was a real Tartar and kept a gun to fire at intruders! As a child she was allowed to pick daffodils on Brownsea.

Her grandparents and uncles were friendly with smugglers who used the house in Dunford Road as a hiding place for goods. They were often visited by Customs men, but the barrels were hidden under the floorboards.

***

Regarding the ghosts, I was told that since the children had grown up and left home, the hauntings had stopped. They were never worried by them though, as they were (to them) obviously their ancestors and meant them no harm. Nevertheless, very interesting houses!

Awareness of death, Runton Road, Parkstone

I was told by a lady who lived there as a child that her brother apparently saw a ghost in their house. They were a happy, united family but the children's much-loved grandfather was very ill. Elizabeth, the eldest child, was aware of this but her three year old brother was not told in case he was upset as he was very close to his grandfather.

At last, the sad news came that grandfather had died. Still the boy was not told, but around the time of the bereavement he was in the hallway and looking up the stairs called out, 'Hello grandad!' He is now a grown man but insists to this day that he saw his grandfather standing there, smiling at him. No-one else saw anything, but perhaps the very young — as well as animals — have a heightened perception of the supernatural!

The 'Visitor', Yarrells Lane, Upton, near Poole

A lady who lives in the lane but who did not want to be identified told me she 'has' a ghost of a woman which is often seen coming up her drive to the house but which never arrives or is seen going away.

There used to be a big wood opposite with a large chicken farm nearby and it was rumoured that the wife of the chicken farmer was 'strange'.

Many people have seen this phantom but she had not witnessed it herself for about 12 months. Other people laughed, telling her it was imagination, but one day one of the 'disbelievers' was with her in the kitchen and told her a woman was coming up the path to her door. She asked her to open it as she was busy, but wasn't surprised when her friend said, 'I distinctly saw someone coming up the drive but there was no-one at the door'.

My informant smiled and said, 'Now YOU have seen "my" ghost!'

The same lady told me of another occasion when she had been looking after her grandson. He had just left and everything was in order in the house. She had finished her meal before going out herself for the evening and then went into her bedroom to change. There, to her amazement she found a large mirror smashed to pieces on the floor. It had been a very heavy, hinged mirror which would have to be lifted to be removed from its setting — and there was no possibility of her young grandson doing that. As she was then alone in the house, she called a neighbour's husband to come and check but there was no sign of a forced entry. Although the smashing of the mirror must have made a terrific crash, she had heard nothing.

The many ghosts of Lytchett Matravers

Lytchett Matravers has several phantoms. The first that was told to me by someone who knew the man involved, was seen in the Old Manor House which, with the exception of the east wing, has now been demolished.

A man who had previously been in the Royal Artillery used to love going to the local dances. One evening in the 1930's he had been to a 'local hop' at Winterbourne and was on his way home at about 3a.m. Full of his evening's conquests, he cheerfully rode his bike through the lanes, whistling dance tunes along the way.

As he approached the Manor, which was unoccupied at the time, he saw a candle being carried in an upstairs room. Surprised, and thinking there may have been intruders, he stopped to watch, dropping his bike by the side of the lane. He stood still for about ten minutes, watching the candle moving silently - and then it vanished. Still thinking there had been a break-in, and being a law-abiding sort of fellow he checked all round the building for a forced entry. Finding everything secure, he returned to his bike. As soon as he picked it up, there was the candle again, floating from room to room.....

Strangely enough, another 'candle' haunting was told me by a previous tenant of Higher Loop Farm, Lytchett Matravers, Freda Maitland. Why 'Loop'? Could it have been the French 'loupe' for a she-wolf? But more of that later!

The lady in question was then a teenager and lived in a tiny cottage near Wimborne Minster with her mother, brothers and sisters. Every now and again a lighted candle would drift up the stairs and disappear into a junk room, but they were never afraid of it.

***

She also told me of the spirit of a grey nun in her habit who, at dawn, was frequently seen crossing the road to the old Grammar School which was founded in 1496. There was a leper hospital nearby in medieval times so perhaps this was from whence the nun originated.

***

When Freda married she lived at Loop Cottage then moved to Higher Loop Farm, (see illustration on the next page) or Loop Manor Farm as it had been centuries ago, when it was part of the great Sturminster Marshall Manor until its division in the 14th century. At that time, a certain Johannes Lhoupe is recorded as living there.

The much-haunted Higher Loop Farm as it used to be prior to modernisation (photograph courtesy of Shirley Percival).

One winter's night, she and her daughter had been to midnight mass on Christmas Eve and were walking home around 12.30–1 a.m. They held each other's arms in the frosty air, chatting about the service, friends in the congregation and the forthcoming festivities.

As they neared the foot of Loop Hill, before them in the moonlight they saw a ghostly white wolf-like animal. They were very frightened as there was no way the beast would let them pass. 'It was certainly no flesh and blood creature', she told me, and instead they made their way home across the fields, petrified and shaking.

When they recounted their experience in the village after Christmas they were told by some of the old folk that the last wolf in the area had been killed at that spot!

***

Higher Loop was fortunate — or unfortunate, depending on your point of view — with its ghosts. The same lady told me about strange noises of

Granny Cook's Cottage, Lytchett Matravers, now demolished. But who - or what - is the shadowy figure on the right? (photograph courtesy of Shirley Percival)

shovelling coal and wood in their pump room, but an inspection next day showed that nothing had been moved.....

***

A ghostly dog was heard barking in Higher Loop farmhouse at night — but at that time they had no dog!

***

The last spectre Freda Maitland told me about was the sound of a lady in a rustling taffeta dress ascending the stairs, walking along the landing and disappearing out of the window. She said her son and daughter used to be terrified when this happened, screaming for their mother. It is believed this unquiet spirit could have been that of a lady living there when it was a Manor farm and who had been murdered in the house by a cowhand.

***

The next Lytchett Matravers ghost is heard in the Church Walk, a path that climbs from the old village that used to be next to the church but was decimated at the time of the Black Death, and now lost beneath the fields. It is said that whispering can be heard just out of sight of the path, but when you look, no-one is there..... Could it be restless spirits of the long-dead plague victims, I wonder?

***

The lovely old church, too, has its wraiths. Back in 1915 a woman cleaner saw a little old lady dressed in the black clothes of a previous era walking slowly up to the altar. She bent her knee in reverence, then moved to a seat near the now bricked up door to the Chantry Chapel, finally kneeling in prayer.

The cleaner, not recognising the stranger watched her intently, then, feeling she was being rude by staring, turned away.

Some impulse made her take another look — but, without passing her, the figure had vanished!

***

On another occasion an old lady (who lived to be 102) had also been alone in the church arranging flowers on the altar when she felt the urge to pray for the soul of the wicked John Maltravers, whose tomb is in the church.

As she finished her prayer she heard a deep, long drawn out sigh from behind her and felt the icy breath on her neck, so close it was.

Terrified, she got to her feet and looked around — but the church was as empty as it had been when she came in.....

The face at the window, Westbourne

Peter Allen told me of a strange thing that happened to him some 20 years ago in Westbourne. He worked then as a self-employed window cleaner and was in a building next to the Westbourne Hotel, opposite the Grand Bingo Hall. On the ground floor there was a yard and a small engineering workshop, while on the floor above there were small rooms let out as offices and workshops to a photographer, an upholsterer and others plus one empty room. His job was to wash down the corridor and stairs once a week and sweep the yard. In the wall above the stairs was a small window to the empty room, which opened outwards.

One day while he was cleaning the stairs he sensed someone watching him. Turning, he glanced up at the little window and saw looking down at him the face of an ugly old man, daubed with white marks. As he watched the window closed. Somewhat shaken, he went into the engineering shop and said to the foreman, 'I thought the office above was empty but I have just seen a man looking out!'

'Of course it's empty' was the reply, 'I've got the only key!'

The next week, to Mr Allen's amazement the same thing happened again: the window opened, the face appeared, then the window closed. He ran downstairs and told the foreman, who brought the key and they both went in. The room was quite empty and the window sill and catch covered in white dust — but there were no fingermarks!

The following week, it happened again but this time a young apprentice was coming downstairs from the toilet. Mr Allen called, 'Look up there!' pointing to the window.

'My God!' cried the boy, and ran! In front of the foreman, Mr Allen questioned the lad as to what he had seen. He wasn't sure, he told them, but it was frightening.

The week after, he asked the foreman to stand under the doorway with his key and he would give him the signal if he saw anything, but that time and on the successive five or six weeks there was nothing.

However, Mr Allen said he never felt comfortable there again so gave up the job. Still curious though, he made enquiries and discovered the place had been stables at the turn of the century, and then a bakehouse for some years. Were the streaks of white on the ugly face flour?

The strange thing was that the face did not appear ethereal but quite solid, just like anyone you would pass in the street. Mr Allen is convinced however that it was not of this world and it made a deep and lasting impression on him.

The building was demolished a few years ago and has been replaced by new offices.

The caring nun, Hamilton Road Orphanage, Boscombe

Once an Orphanage run by nuns, these premises are now a block of flats for elderly people — but that does not mean the children or the nuns have departed!

There is a plaque on the wall giving details of its previous usage and I am told that several of the present inhabitants have described hearing footsteps in the corridors, as long-dead nuns check the dormitories to see if their tender charges are safe.

Someone who visited the flats told me she always felt uneasy in one of the corridors, 'As though something else was there with me', she said, and would hurry along it as quickly as she could to reach the safety of the flats which, thankfully, do not seem to be disturbed.

The ghost that scared the Bournemouth plumber

In his younger days John Shave of Bournemouth was a plumber. One morning an estate agent telephoned and asked him to fix a damaged wash basin in an unoccupied house in the town.

Arriving at the house complete with his radio and toolbag, he immediately noticed a strange feeling of depression in the atmosphere, but put it down to the house being vacant for a long period.

He climbed the stairs to a bedroom facing them, where he had been told the wash basin was situated and placed his toolbag on the floor. Before starting work he decided to visit the toilet and whilst he was in there heard heavy footsteps coming up the stairs.

Thinking it was his boss, he called out 'I'm up here' but there was no answer. Puzzled, he searched the whole of the upper floor and finding no-one examined the ground floor as well — but the house was empty! He shook his head, knowing what he had heard, but then thought that it may have been a tramp as the house had been empty for so long, and who had beaten a hasty retreat when he heard someone was there.

John went back upstairs to get on with the repairs and switching on his radio (without which no plumber can work!) he began selecting the tools for the job.

Suddenly he felt the room grow icy cold (it was mid-summer) and felt something was 'not quite right' as he put it. Getting to his feet he felt the coldness surrounding him like a fog and knew he was not alone. Although he could see no apparition he was fully aware that it was there.

He called out loudly, 'I am a plumber, here to see to the damaged basin!' and felt the wraith standing right in front of him. He continued, 'Now, if you will allow me to get on with this job I will not interfere with you and when it is finished I will go and leave you in peace!'

The seconds ticked away and gradually the cold atmosphere seeped from the room on to the landing. The room regained its normal temperature and the radio (which had lost its volume) became clear again.

Shakily, the plumber rolled a much-needed cigarette, lit up and got on with the job.

Repairs complete, he stood on the landing and called out, 'The job is finished and I am leaving you now. I promise I will not return' — a promise which plumber John Shave was only too happy to keep!

New Street Poole, the footsteps on the stairs

A similar haunting happened in Poole when two old cottages were being converted into one.

A workman installing a boiler in a cupboard near the foot of the stairs heard footsteps ascending the staircase. He called out, thinking it was a fellow workman and when there was no reply, explored the top storey — only to find the house unoccupied. One room however had a strangely cold atmosphere and other people who had worked there experienced the same chill. The phantom — if that was what it was — became known to those who visited as 'Harry', but why, I have been unable to discover.

Worth Matravers' benevolent vicar

The lovely old stone cottage where the next ghost appeared was built in 1640 in the village of Worth Matravers, and was possibly the original rectory. I was told of the sighting by the lady who lives there and up until his appearance she was very sceptical about ghosts. Although she only saw him once, she told me he was very real to her.

Her husband was ill in hospital so she was alone in the kitchen preparing her supper. Turning, she saw a figure with very dark hair standing inside her gate and she had the impression that he was a clergyman. From her window he was only visible from the waist up and he seemed to be wearing a dark top, a wide black leather belt and a clerical collar. She shook her head, telling herself it was figment of the imagination and turned back to the stove.

A little later, she moved towards the door, glancing out of the window as she passed and there was the figure again, coming down her path. As he approached her window he looked at her and smiled, giving her the impression of a kindly, caring face ... then he vanished before her eyes!

The lady told me she wasn't in the least frightened as he seemed a benevolent spirit. Perhaps he was reassuring her about her husband? Who knows!

Hamworthy's ghosts

I was told of the ghost of a gardener who did not want to leave his garden. It appeared on a garden seat of an old house in Hamworthy where an old man used to look after the garden. Several people have seen it and all believe it to be the one-time gardener of the house. It is a harmless old spectre, who just sits there, contemplating his old 'haunts' then fades away.

***

Another Hamworthy spectre is said to whistle for his lady-love! Unfortunately, (and somewhat naturally!) her husband did not approve of this liaison and, discovering the pair together, shot them both, throwing the lover's body into a nearby pond. Undeterred, his ghost can still be heard giving the same curious whistle with which he called his lady-love.

Amesbury — the conscientious pharmacist

A lady who used to work in the shop twenty-four years ago related the following to me:

She had been standing at the hatch to the pharmacy with a prescription to hand to the chemist when she noticed he was apparently engaged with what she took to be a 'rep'. The 'rep' was a tall man in a navy blue suit and, not wanting to interrupt them, she walked away.

A few moments later she checked again, as the prescription was urgent and saw the man was no longer there.

'Has the gentleman left?' she asked another assistant.

'What gentleman?' was the reply.

'The one with Mr X' she answered.

'He didn't have anyone with him' said her colleague.

About an hour later my informant was talking to the other assistant again and said, 'I must have been seeing things just now. I thought there was a tall man in a navy blue suit with Mr X!'

'Oh no,' said her colleague with a smile, 'that would have been Mr Y. Everybody sees him! He was the previous pharmacist and loved his work. He was always here and since he died it seems he still can't keep away!'

The strange man of Marler House, Westbourne

This ghost appeared in a modern several-storied office block, but it was the house which was previously on the site to which it 'belonged'.

The same lady who told me about the Dunford Road hauntings used to have a cleaning job in Marler House. Sometimes her son would help her and as they finished an office they would turn off the lights.

One day when they were the only two people left in the building her son asked her who was the strange man in the corner. He had said hello to him but was ignored. His mother asked what the man looked like and was told he was very tall with a cloak and tall hat. As her son described him he realised he was indeed strange!

They returned home and my informant mentioned what they had seen to her mother who said, 'Oh yes, that was Dr X who lived in the old house that used to be there'.

'How do you know?' asked her daughter.

'I used to live in that house, and I was a receptionist for Dr X' her mother replied. Until that moment her daughter had not known that was where she worked, although she knew of her job as a receptionist.

The ghost only appeared on that one occasion, possibly through the family connection of grandmother, mother and son? Another case of 'Getting the right conditions'?

The Royal Oak, Bere Regis

Pubs, especially long-established ones seem to have their fair share of ghosts, the Royal Oak being no exception.

Theirs is known as 'John' and several people have seen him — 'A misty, dark figure,' as one of the regulars at the bar described him to me. Pictures fall from walls with the cord still attached to the hanger, glasses topple without being touched — and the floor is perfectly level! Another elderly regular, known as 'Buddy L' (because of the times he uses the expression) said he once felt the air become very cold and believed he was in the presence of 'John' — but he wouldn't look around in case he was!

On another occasion a barmaid, who has since left, was in the cellar when she sensed someone behind her. Thinking it was the landlord, she spoke to him but received no reply. On turning, she saw a dark, misty presence and hurried back upstairs. She asked the landlord if he had been down to the cellar, but neither he nor anyone else had left the bar. From that time until she left, the barmaid would not go down the cellar unless she was accompanied. In spite of that, everyone else agreed he was not a frightening spectre but could give no clue as to his identity. So 'John' remains a mystery.

Pudding and Pye Inn, Wimborne

There is a glass door to the rear of this pub but often tenants were disturbed by a loud knocking on the WOODEN door which it replaced. On answering the knock — at their GLASS door — they found no-one was there. They called in a friend one night to try and solve the mystery. He stood by the door, waiting for the knock. Suddenly the telephone rang and the landlady went to answer it. Then came the knock on the 'wooden' door and a voice called softly, 'Jean', (the landlady's name) but there was no-one at the door, or on the telephone.

No-one could give any explanation for this happening. The pub now has a new landlord and the knocks appear to have ceased.

***

Wattles Hotel, Hythe

The following case is similar to the one of the Dunford Road, Parkstone hauntings:

A previous tenant often noticed a strong but pleasant perfume around this old hotel, reminiscent of freesias. There was no logical explanation for this, but it kept occurring.

Later it transpired that many years ago there had been a nursery to the rear of the hotel — where they specialised in ... freesias!

Cornwall Hotel, Dorchester

From time to time there are inexplicable happenings at this public house. The landlord believes the culprits are American servicemen who were billeted there prior to D-Day in the Second World War and whose spirits still play pranks.

One evening after closing time the family and a friend were seated around the very realistic log-effect gas fire they have in the public bar (see illustration opposite). The landlord told me they talked in a relaxed manner, gazing into the flickering flames, the only control of which was a rather stiff key which was in full sight of everyone.

As they sat yarning away as one will in a pub, even after the customers have departed, the flames of the 'logs' suddenly shot up, remained high for a minute or so then the flames were extinguished .... without the help of a human hand the stiff key had moved and turned off the gas!

They looked at each other in puzzled amazement. How could it have happened! No-one had touched the key and the landlord could give me no explanation for the event.

***

Things frequently go missing in the pub's living quarters, again with no obvious explanation. One item to 'disappear' was a training shoe which turned up some few days later where no-one had put it, with the laces knotted and knotted again in a strange pattern.

***

There is a table for two in the public bar which is alongside an old church-like fresco. On the table was a special 'sputter proof' candle from a batch the landlord had bought and on which the wax did not run.

One day, an American visitor sat at this particular table. The candle took on a life of its own, sputtering and wax running like a thing demented. Had the long-departed spirits recognised a fellow American I wonder, and decided to play a trick?

On another occasion, the landlord was in the cellar where there is a sump that slowly fills and empties with water. The sump was full one minute — then the next it was empty — an impossibility! He did not loiter in the cellar as it 'felt strange' but left the task he had begun for another day.

***

In 1994 the Brewery decided they would redecorate the pub. All went well until one morning when the decorators returned and found scrawling scratch marks some ten feet up the wall on the paper they had hung the previous day, as though made by two hands or pairs of claws.

The decorator asked the landlord to keep his bull terrier under control as it had spoilt the paper, but he said it couldn't possibly have reached that height — and the dog had not been in that room in any case!

The fireplace in the Cornwall Hotel.

Were these events too caused by the spirits of the long-dead Americans? Who knows!

Postscript

I was sitting in the Cornwall Hotel with my cousin Edith, who was staying with me, a few weeks after writing this. We had just finished an excellent meal and were lingering over our coffee when I mentioned that I was writing this book, and that the hotel had a ghost.

As I mentioned the word 'ghost' Edith said, 'Did you see that?'

'What?' I asked.

'The candle on the table,' she laughed. 'The flame grew higher when you said 'ghost'!'

I was looking at the flame as she spoke — and the same thing happened again! We both laughed and I moved the candle further away from us in case our breath was affecting it. Those on the other tables were behaving quite normally, giving the odd flicker but nothing more sinister.

Edith experimented, saying words like 'toast' and 'boast' but nothing happened. Whenever she said 'ghost' however the flame grew taller! We laughed again, perhaps a little uneasily this time.

'I'll give it a test' Edith said cunningly and addressed the candle. 'If you are a real ghost, grow smaller and if you are not, grow taller.' THE FLAME GREW SMALLER!

I added more cream to my coffee so I could finish it quickly and we went to the bar to pay. I told Steve Evans the landlord what had happened and he just smiled wryly. Kirsty his daughter said unconcernedly, 'Yes, we DO have ghosts here!'

The True Lover's Knot, Tarrant Keynston

This attractive old pub is on the road from Blandford to Badbury Rings, and according to the current tenants the previous landlord and his predecessors both experienced a friendly poltergeist.

Pictures in one of the bedrooms would change places without the assistance of human hands and the lights would go on and off by themselves.

One day the landlord found himself locked in the cellar when 'something' slid the bolt across.

Another day, he was again in the cellar when he became aware of a hissing sound. Curious, he searched for its source and discovered a spare gas cylinder for the beer pumps was turned on and the gas escaping. It had been there undisturbed for weeks previously and no-one had touched it.

Nevertheless, the poltergeist — if that was what it was — had never caused any real damage, purely mischief! A spook with a sense of fun...?

***

Although most of the hauntings so far have been in private houses or pubs, the following are reports from historic houses:

The phantoms of Smedmore House

Lying in a valley in the beautiful Purbeck Hills is Smedmore House. Built in the early 17th century by Sir William Clavell and remodelled in the next century it is sometimes opened to the public and well worth a visit, as nowadays the atmosphere is both friendly and welcoming. The occurrences which follow were told to me by Major J C Mansel whose son now lives there.

Major Mansel's parents moved to Smedmore in 1925 and learned of a curious happening in 1833 concerning the death in mysterious circumstances of the Reverend John Clavell, the then owner of Smedmore Estate.

The old man had become a recluse, seeing little of his relatives, and keeping them in the dark as to how he would dispose of his property. When it became known that he was very ill, Colonel John Mansel, whose wife Louise was the Reverend John Clavell's niece and next of kin, galloped over to Smedmore, hoping to see the old man before he died.

When the Colonel arrived the housekeeper leaned out of a bedroom window crying, 'You're too late, he's dead!' and slammed the window down.

The Mansel family searched the house for a will but found nothing. However, about three months later the daughter of the housekeeper produced a will which left nearly everything to her fiance, the bailiff, which she said had been kept hidden on the old man's instructions.

Naturally enough, the Mansels disputed the will, which the Courts declined to accept and in due course Louise succeeded to the property.

***

It is said that periodically a window in Smedmore House would slam down without warning, repeating what happened when Colonel Mansel galloped up to the house.

Also, inexplicable rumblings were heard in the attics and this was said to be the spirit of the housekeeper angrily shifting her furniture when she had to leave.

There were also reports by a family who rented the house prior to 1925 of a 'little old man in a snuff-coloured waistcoat' who was said to appear at a certain place at a certain time.

Major Mansel told me that a member of the family used to sit up at night with his watch in his hand waiting for the appointed time, hoping to see this apparition but he doesn't know if he ever succeeded!

Since the installation of electric lighting though, no ghosts have ever been seen or heard of again.

The ghosts of Athelhampton

Athelhampton House is famous for its beauty and despite a recent disastrous fire is now lovingly restored to its former glory. Standing in magnificent gardens laid out in the late 19th century, parts of the house date back to 1493, built for the Martyn family whose emblem was a monkey. One of these animals belonged to the family in the 16th century and can be seen in the coat of arms in the stained glass windows. The family crest shows a monkey with a looking glass and the enigmatic words, 'He who looks at Martyn's ape, Martyn's ape shall look at him'.

When the line petered out in 1595 it is said that the pet monkey roamed the house searching for its new master, only to find four surviving daughters and no heir. Scratching noises can be heard behind the panelling in the Great Chamber as the monkey's wraith tries in vain to escape from the secret staircase and cellar.

The present owner, Patrick Cooke, also told me of a ghostly cooper who taps away at barrels in the wine cellar which is reached from the Great Hall, and where two duellists can be heard clashing their swords at evening time. They are believed to date back to the Civil War when the house had Royalist connections.

***

The Chapel too has its ghost — a hooded monk who wanders from room to room as though he still lives in the house.

***

The spirit of a Grey Lady passes through the walls from the landing to the Tudor Bedroom and Yellow Bedroom. Once she was seen by a housemaid, who, thinking she was a visitor remaining after the house was closed for the day, asked her to leave. Obediently the spectre rose and disappeared through the panelling!

***

Other spirits remain in the house although no-one knows who they are. Written on the stone entrance to the Library are the words, 'Once I loved no one but Then I loved M...' and a date 1660.

***

Athelhampton House is open to the public April to October from 12 noon to 5 p.m. on Tuesdays, Wednesdays, Thursdays, Sundays and Bank Holidays. Also Mondays and Fridays in July and August. It is on the A35, 5 miles east of Dorchester.

Lord Digby's servant's apparition, Calne

The mother of a girl I knew as a child was in service with Lord Digby near Calne in the 1920's.

One evening she was in her room in the servants' quarters when she saw 'an apparition' drift across the room at the foot of her bed. 'Mrs M' was in her 80's when I last saw her and not in the best of health but her son told me she always described it without any variation over the years. There must have been several sightings in view of what followed, as the interesting part was that the gardener discovered a window to an unknown room, next to the servant girl's. This was opened up and the room eventually exorcised.

The author at Rockbourne Roman Villa in the 1950s.

Weird happenings at Rockbourne Roman Villa

Back in the 1950s and 1960s on every Sunday from Spring to Autumn my friend Joan Davies and I would catch the number 38 Wilts and Dorset bus from Bournemouth to Fordingbridge. There, Morley Hewitt, discoverer and owner of the Rockbourne Roman Villa would meet us in his old Armstrong Siddley car and take us to the Villa where we, along with several other 'diggers' were excavating the site. (see illustration)

We were a happy bunch, rigging up makeshift tents of plastic if it should rain and sweltering in our shorts when the sun shone. Morley jokingly referred to us as his 'slaves'. Trowelling, bucketing, sifting and barrowing we worked like them, too — but willingly and our reward was in our work.

The Villa became our *raison d'être* and one day Joan and I decided we would travel on Saturday and spend the weekend there to give us more time on the site. People sometimes did this, but we had never tried it before.

Equipped with sleeping bags and sandwiches we cadged a lift with a woman from Bournemouth who usually dug on Saturdays, as we had too much gear to take on the bus. We worked all day, revelling in the extra time and then at last evening came. Waving goodbye to the team we went into the prefabricated (as it was then) museum. There was a small room at the rear where boxes of shards and small finds were kept prior to classification and we spread our sleeping bags on the floor. Recalling the events of the day's dig, we had a last walk around the site before turning in. Dew cooled the grass and it was pleasant to have the place to ourselves. The old yew tree over by the Roman Ditch (it was known by that name long before the Villa was rediscovered — strange how long folk memories can last) darkened against the evening sky and we decided it was time for bed.

There was no electric light in the museum in those days but we had a candle, and the moon was bright. It wasn't too bad on the floor and, tired after our physical exertions of the day, we were soon asleep.

***

It must have been around midnight when I was suddenly aware of a dreadful feeling of what I can only describe as evil, as though something terrible had happened or was about to happen. It came in through one wall and hung over us like a mist. I was completely paralysed. All I could do was lie there and wait!

After what seemed ages but was probably only a few minutes, the feeling began to fade. My limbs regained their power.

I whispered, 'Joan! Are you awake?'

'Yes!' she replied.

'I've just had the most awful dream!' I told her.

'Don't talk about it now,' she pleaded, 'Wait until it's daylight!'

We didn't go back to sleep. There was a small transistor radio in the little office and we switched it on, changing stations as they closed down and finding another, just to keep in touch with the real world.

About half way through the night as we lay there on the floor a strange creaking sound came from outside — like waggon wheels turning! We looked at each other in the dim moonlight and giggled hysterically, diving down into our sleeping bags and covering our faces in fear.

As the first light of day filtered through the window I told Joan about my dream.

She looked at me strangely. 'I had that feeling, at the VERY SAME TIME!' she said quietly.

Thinking back, we must have been mad, never giving a thought to the possibility of anything supernatural when we decided to sleep there. Surrounded as we were by personal belongings of the Villa's occupants, plus two skeletons of babies which had been buried beneath the floor — it was surely asking for trouble. Then there was Fred the Saxon who had been robbing rooftiles from the then deserted Villa when the wooden supports gave way. Dying alone and un-sought for, we found his skeleton with a broken back centuries later. His remains were in a box on a shelf, his skull which was kept together by a modern plaster bandage fixed in a grin of final death agony.

Yet somehow these did not seem to be the source of the 'aura' as I can best describe it, as it entered from outside, hovered, then moved away again apparently unconnected with the museum's artifacts.

Daylight came and, thankfully, we dressed, went outside and saw to our intense relief the wooden door of the tool shed stood open!

'Our waggon wheels explained, at least!' I said breathing a grateful sigh.

The Sunday diggers began to arrive and we were soon relating our experiences.

One old bachelor often slept in the car park in his car. Yes, there WAS something strange, he told us — but nothing would induce him to go into details.

Another local digger told us that some years before he used to go courting on his bicycle along the road between Sandleheath and Rockbourne. For some strange reason, whenever he came to the place where the Villa had yet to be discovered he would lower his head and pedal like mad! There was something weird in the atmosphere, he told us. But what it was, we will probably never know — the Villa still holds its mysteries.

***

One last twist, however. We told our fellow-diggers about the 'waggon wheels' and I laughed, saying 'You can imagine our relief when we saw this shed door was open,' moving it to demonstrate.

THE DOOR DID NOT CREAK...!

The Church in the Rings, Knowlton

Peter Briggs of Broadstone told me of an experience he had in his mid teens during the late 1950s.

On the day of Cranborne Summer Carnival he had cycled all the way from Broadstone for a day's outing. In the evening, the festivities were over and he was returning home on his bicycle when he decided to break his journey at Knowlton Church in the Rings.

Dating from ancient times, the church was abandoned following the Black Death of 1348 when the population of Knowlton Village was decimated and is now a ruin.

At the time when Peter was there the Bronze Age Rings were overgrown with trees and bushes, not cleared as they are now. So, late on that still summer's evening he pushed his way through the undergrowth then to his horror heard a great crashing and thrashing around as though a herd of cows had run amok — but there were no animals there — only himself — and whatever caused the noise!

There are legends of witchcraft relating to the site and several others have reported an unearthly chill in the remains of the church, but whatever the real cause was — we may never know.

The voices of Tilly Whim Caves

Peter Briggs also told me of an experience he had as a boy in Purbeck. This was after Tilly Whim Caves were closed to the public as unsafe. As youths will, he found a way into the caves over a wall, avoiding the locked and barred entrance.

Waves crashed on the rocks below but he was where no one had stood for many a day. Elated, he was exploring the caves, alone in the gloom, when he swears he heard muffled conversations coming from the depths. Were they the voices of long-dead smugglers who were known to use the caves, or even the quarrymen who laboured there beneath the overhanging rocks? Who knows? Peter said he didn't wait to find out!

The man on the bicycle, Longham

Mrs Whitely of Bear Cross told me that she didn't believe in ghosts, but she couldn't explain what she had seen any other way.

On 11th April 1994 at 9.35 p.m. she was going to work at Ferndown and had just crossed over Longham Bridge. Between there and the Bridge House Hotel she saw a man in a long macintosh on an old fashioned bicycle — rather like the ones policemen used to ride — without any lights on the wrong side of the road.

As she looked at him, thinking 'That's dangerous!' a white car approached - and drove right through him!

Arriving at her place of work, her colleagues noticed how pale she seemed and said she looked as though she had seen a ghost.

'I have!' she replied.

For a couple of days she still felt shaken, as this was something entirely outside her experience and she didn't know what to believe. She said the apparition had been elderly, with a long neck. She saw him quite clearly.

Does anyone know of an accident at this spot and could identify the apparition? I would pleased if you would tell me.

'Annie' of Riverside Mews, Mill Lane, Wimborne

I was given the following information by the previous owner, who believed 'their' ghost was that of Annie, a 15 year old girl who had worked for the miller many years ago.

The 18th century mill was on the River Allen, the present site of their coffee lounge, and the girl used to take the miller his supper each evening. She was a pretty, mischievous little thing, perhaps flirting with the older miller until one day, overcome with lust, he raped her.

Distraught, she ran away from him, tripped and fell into the millstream, hitting her head, losing consciousness and was drowned.

My informant who gave up the premises in July 1994 told me she had seen the apparition twice in the last couple of years. Her last sighting was when she was in the kitchen with her husband — who saw nothing.

The ghost put its head round the door and greeted her. Thinking it was one of the girls who worked there she went to see what had happened to her as she hadn't reappeared — but there was no coat hanging in the hall and no sign of her staff!

Sometimes small handbells which were on the tables in the restaurant would ring of their own accord, or someone would call her name, but again there was no-one there.

An old-fashioned doll used to be kept on the sideboard in the restaurant. Her son was passing, carrying a tray when of its own volition the doll suddenly flew through the air and landed on the floor!

There was a certain place in the wall of the premises where my informant's dog used to scratch and whine. The owners took no notice, assuming it to be after mice but then heard there used to a door in that spot and other dogs had howled and refused to pass it. Perhaps it was Annie's door?

On another occasion, five of them were in the kitchen. Plates came off the side, hovered then smashed on the floor to the amazement of the onlookers. They were dumbfounded — but put it down to Annie's mischief and often spoke to her. Things were moved around, and however often they were replaced would be found back again where 'Annie' had put them. Electric plugs would be found out of their sockets and the coffee machine turned off.

One year, they put on a 'Victorian Christmas' but Annie threw the menu cards across the floor with an impish sense of humour.

In general, no-one found Annie a problem, but one day an extra sensitive customer came in and took her seat at a table. After a short space of time she said, 'I'm sorry, I've got to go out. I've got a horrible feeling I'm being watched from behind!' and left. She had been there before and since with no problems, but on that occasion her mind was 'in tune' with Annie's mischievous spirit.

Mount Talbot Cottage, Alder Road, Parkstone. Now demolished - but were the noises caused by ghosts - or smugglers?

One weekend, my informant went away leaving a very down to earth French girl in charge — but, being in the restaurant on her own, she experienced a feeling of dread and couldn't stay.

The regular staff, however, didn't mind Annie although they sometimes had the feeling when washing up, if they turned around they would see someone — but they never had the courage to do so!

The gypsy's phantom devil horse

I was told by a gypsy who lived in a caravan at Burgess Field, Parkstone as a child, that she and her brother believed their caravan had been visited by a horse-like devil!

It was broad daylight and they were both inside the caravan — a traditional one with half-doors — when a black, velvety 'thing' with wild eyes and red, snorting nostrils glared at them over the half-door, putting the fear of God into them.

Terrified, they called for their parents who were outside at the time but had seen nothing. Neither were there any hoofprints on the soft turf .... but the children knew what THEY had seen!

34

The Alder Hills smugglers?

Until 1988, prior to the new Sainsbury's being built on Alder Hills at Parkstone, there was an old cottage known as 'Mount Talbot' or 'Mount Ararat' on top of the hill. The latter name was from a time when the area was flooded and the cottage rose like Noah's Ark from the waters.

It was built around 1810 (see illustration), and rumour had it that on wild, stormy nights strange figures could be seen around the cottage, with weird cries and groans coming from its walls.

Needless to say, folk kept their distance .... which was probably just as well as the cottage (which was reputedly used to store contraband) was on the smugglers' route from Canford Cliffs to Kinson, and I have been told by a descendant of one that this 'trade' continued well into the 20th century.

Bygone children's voices of the old Dorset school

These 'happenings' were described by the Headmaster of a Dorset school which has now moved to new, modern premises.

Before the move, he was working late at the school one evening. The task finished, he let himself out of the building, locking the door behind him. Moonlight shone across the playground and surrounding fields when, crossing to his car, he became aware of the sound of children's voices happily at play. Wondering what they were doing so late in the evening, he searched the area — but no-one was there.

On another occasion he was working late again, but this time was accompanied by the husband of one of the teachers. As before, on leaving the building they heard the sound of children at play — but there WERE no children! Since that time repeatedly they have been heard again, but only on moonlit nights.

In the staffroom one day the Headmaster mentioned the uncanny sounds to another of the teachers whose garden backed on to the school and she said she too had heard the children from time to time. There was nothing frightening about it, just spirits from a bygone age, still playing happily together.

The man who met himself coming back!

Adrian Brown of Winton saw his doppelganger (legendary ghostly double of a living person) whilst driving the van of a local security firm he worked for. It happened in 1990 as he was checking various sites in the area for his firm.

Not a gullible man — he has a technology degree and a deep understanding of philosophy — he was driving around a roundabout near Holton Heath when, on the opposite side he saw the firm's identical van — with HIMSELF driving it! The other 'him' turned his head and their eyes met. Adrian told me he couldn't clearly describe the uneasy feeling he had at that moment. It started in the pit of his stomach and he had never experienced anything like it before. The strange thing was, he was running late, having been delayed at one of the sites and the other 'him' was where he would have been if he hadn't been held up.

It was a couple of days before he could sort out his thoughts as his brain felt numb. His firm DID have another van — but no, that wasn't the explanation — THAT van had broken down and was off the road.

Adrian had read of parallel universes, a theory of modern physics and said, 'What if I'm not really here and the guy driving the other van is the real Adrian!'

A frightening thought!

The vanishing boy, near Sidmouth

This next tale was told to me by Lady Phyllis Bell of Bournemouth.

During the summer of 1994 she had been on a day trip by coach to Sidmouth where she spent a very pleasant day in glorious weather.

At 4.00 pm the coach set off back to Bournemouth and soon after leaving Sidmouth it climbed a long hill with a right hand bend at the top. She was sitting well back in the coach on the right hand side as the coach rounded the bend so had a good view of the road ahead.

To her horror, standing on the white line in the middle of the road and facing the coach was a young boy! Before she could collect her wits to cry out to the driver, 'Mind that child!' the coach had passed the spot — and the driver had taken no notice!

Lady Bell said she had a very clear view of the boy. He was about nine years old, with grey knee socks, brown shoes, a dark green blazer with a yellow badge on the breast pocket, matching green school cap again with the yellow badge and grey shorts. He was a lovely looking little boy with rosy cheeks — in fact a typical young schoolboy of a couple of decades ago.

On reaching Bournemouth, Lady Bell enquired of the driver, the outings organiser and other passengers in the front of the coach — but no-one else had seen him!

Could he have been the victim of a road accident some years ago? If anyone has an answer to this or recognises the school uniform, PLEASE let me know. My informant and I are both intrigued!

The phantom of 'Sally in the Wood', Monkton Farleigh

During the Second World War, Mr Skerman of Branksome was in the War Department Police at Monkton Farleigh, which is about six miles from Bath.

One night, he was on duty at the ammunition sidings and went into the little hut which was used for tea-breaks by the ammunition lorry drivers.

Suddenly the door was flung open and a driver staggered in in a terrible state.

'What's the matter?' cried Mr Skerman with concern, as the fellow was white and shaking. The man couldn't speak for some time, then gradually regained his composure.

'I was coming from Monkton Farleigh through the trees', he began, the cup of tea which had been thrust into his hands spilling as he shook. 'You know, where the ammo dump that's 100 foot underground is, by 'Sally in the Wood'. (This was the name by which the wooded area was known locally.)

'I had just entered the wood when a little old lady who was standing in the middle of the road stopped my lorry. I KNOW we're not supposed to stop by law when we are carrying ammo, but what could I do? I couldn't drive right over her, could I?' he said, near to tears, appealing to his mates.

It appeared that without speaking the little old lady indicated that she wanted a lift. The driver opened the door and she climbed in, sitting beside him. He drove on down the Bath Ford road until he reached the turning for the ammunition sidings where he stopped. Looking towards his passenger to tell her she must alight before anyone saw he had given her a lift, to his utter amazement there was no-one there!

Mr Skerman told me that he later learned she was the 'Sally' of 'Sally in the Wood', an old woman whose spectre haunted her old home. He said he had never seen anyone as terrified as that driver in all his life!

Poole High Street Murders, 1598

(From *High Street Murders 1598* by Patricia M Wilnecker and published by Poole Museums)

I discovered this story when transcribing documents in the Archives of the Borough of Poole in 1980. There were some forty pages of statements and eye witness accounts of the murders, and the words which echo down the centuries were the actual ones used 400 years ago but I have used modern spelling for clarity.

Many years ago, in 1598 to be exact, a widow Mistress Alice Greene lived in Scaplens Court at the bottom of Poole High Street. Her late husband

William had been a wealthy merchant, shipowner and five times Mayor of Poole. On his death most of his wealth went to his widow Alice, who lived alone except for two little dogs and her maidservant Agnes Beard.

Their daughter Joane lived next door with her husband John Beryman, merchant and owner of the Three Mariners Inn and who had also served as Poole's Mayor in 1595, so the families were well known in the town which like so many others was much smaller in those days.

News of Alice's inheritance soon spread around the alehouses, and Agnes the faithful maidservant was visited by a friend who came to talk about it. She disclosed there had been a 'scene' between her mistress and Beryman who said he was dissatisfied with his share of the will, swearing he would 'have more before he had done'. This had greatly upset Agnes who said to her friend, 'I pray to God I may live no longer than my Mistress' — LITTLE REALISING HOW SOON AND IN WHAT DREADFUL MANNER THIS PLEA WAS TO BE REALISED!

Christmas came and went and on the evening of Twelfth Night Goodman Dibbon was passing Alice's house when he heard the little dogs barking furiously — then suddenly they were quiet. Someone was carrying a light upstairs from the hall to the bedchamber, but he thought no more about it until next day.

Evening came and nothing had been seen of Alice or her maid, so worried friends helped a youth through a little window in the staircase. He squeezed in, then the small crowd in the street heard the lad scream, 'MURDER!'. In panic the townspeople forced the door with an iron bar finding Alice, Agnes and the two little dogs lying dead in pools of blood. All had been battered about the head with a pressing iron then stabbed with a dagger.

Eventually the case came to court and several men were suspected of carrying out the foul deed: Gowin Spencer who lived near St James churchyard with wife Elioner and 9 year old daughter Gerrard; Roberte Hill of Poole; Clement Starre whose tenement overlooked Alice's courtyard; Richard Parminter servant of John Beryman — and John Beryman himself!

Giving evidence, Elioner Spencer told the court that on the day of the murders her husband Gowin had been abroad in the town until 8 of the clock. She had buttered fish for his supper and asked him why he was so late. Ignoring the question he told her to have her supper as he couldn't eat anything. Then she spotted what she took to be a stewed prune clinging to the back of his stocking but touching it, found it was a thick clot of blood. He explained it away by saying it was the result of a nose bleed. Elioner then discovered his cloak was also bloody but he took it from her, washing both it and his stockings himself and some days later having the cloak dyed black at Wimborne.

Next morning Elioner rose early and went outside for kindling. As she was lighting the fire her husband asked her what news she had heard in the town. 'Nothing' she replied. Then he told her he had brought home forty shillings the night before and asked her to go to the market and buy some butter. There she heard Agnes Beard had been murdered. On telling her husband, he said, 'So is Mistress Greene killed, too!'.

Realising he was implicated she cried, 'You have undone yourself and us all!'.

'Hold thy peace!' he shouted, 'or else by God I will knock thy head against the wall!'.

Some time later he disclosed to her that Roberte Hill had committed the murder, and gave her the dagger that he had made round and sharp and which unwittingly she used the garden.

It appeared that Gowin Spencer, Roberte Hill and Richard Parminter had the key to John Beryman's cellar which opened a door to a passage leading into Alice's house. From the entry they went directly into a little room under the stairs where they lay in wait for Alice. She put up a fight, struggling with Spencer, pulling away a piece of his beard, 'skin and all'. Hill struck her on the head and then Spencer stabbed her, leaving the woman lying dead on the floor. The men crept to the hall where Alice was sitting at supper, unaware of the horror in the other room. They leaped in, battering her about the head with an iron, then stabbing her, brutally killing her and the two little dogs, to stop them raising the alarm.

With the only witnesses out of the way they took a candle and went upstairs to the chamber, breaking open a wooden chest belonging to Alice, dividing the money and jewels between them.

The murderers were on the point of leaving when they heard a loud knocking on the door. They stood stock still, looking at each other in fear, hardly daring to breath then Gowin whispered, 'Oh Lord, we shall all be taken!'.

At last they heard the footsteps going away and quickly left by the street door.

There had also been some documents in the chest which the conspirators took to John Beryman who was obviously expecting them. Asking the men what they had done, they replied, 'Murdered Agnes Beard and the old woman!'. His heartless reply was that he would not have had them kill the old woman, showing no concern for her maidservant.

The men later sold the jewels at Woodbury Hill Fair near Bere Regis but John Beryman kept some of the documents. Unfortunately, what was in them we shall probably never know. What we DO know is that Beryman had given Elioner a new red flannel petticoat as a bribe, telling her to speak no more of the murders to anyone.

***

It was a strange court case, four hundred years ago. Only Roberte Hill was hanged for the murders but as the accounts are not complete we do not know the full story. The actual words of the participants are recorded in documents that remain in the town archives however, making fascinating reading.

***

It could be — and it seems likely — that the woman in grey, wearing an apron crossing the courtyard of Scaplens Court and then climbing the stairs is the unquiet spirit of the maidservant Agnes Beard. She has been described by a previous museum attendant (15th century Scaplens Court is now a museum) as 'floating', while a current attendant was aware of a 'cold presence and uncomfortable feeling as though someone was behind you' in the old room behind the solar.

Is she forever trying to warn her mistress of the intruders? There are also mysterious sounds of dogs barking ... where there are no dogs!

If you are ever in Poole on Twelfth Night and are brave enough to wait quietly outside Scaplens Court, who knows what you may hear and see!!

The Market Street hauntings, Poole

Market Street in Poole seems to have more than its fair share of hauntings. It is, however, one of the oldest streets in the town, being shown on the earliest recorded street plans so I suppose if anywhere is to have a ghost, this is one of the most likely areas (see illustration).

I was told the next story by an architect who lived there.

'One night', he told me, 'a very strange thing happened. My son had been home on vacation, writing one of his theses. He liked to work in the spare bedroom which was used as library/workroom and had gone out for the evening with a friend while I started work renovating a staircase, removing paint from the Victorian balusters.'

He continued working on one of them for a couple of hours and still it was not finished.

'I'm going to bed early,' said his wife as she passed by, 'I'm getting a shocking cold. You'd better put up the bed in the spare room — don't want to catch it, do you?'

He agreed and went on working, taking about another fifteen minutes to complete the job.

The pine looked lovely and he couldn't resist running his fingers over the silkiness of the wood, thinking he might have been the first person to have touched the actual baluster in two hundred years.

He stroked the pine again, but now, as his fingers moved down the shaft of the miniature Tuscan column so icy hands caressed his spine, moving endlessly.

'It was horrible!' he told me. He went straight to the bathroom, turned on the hot tap, stripped and got in feeling a sense of relief as the heat of the water restored him to normality.

In bed, he felt better and must have slept until the early hours when suddenly, without warning, heavy iron-clad boots clobbered clumsily overhead! Strong men struggled to move heavy chests, turning them on their

Market Street, Poole, where many hauntings have been reported.

corners, grinding in the gritty dust, splintering the boards and occasionally losing control, crashing the chests to the floor. He heard the men's boots clattering as they lost their footing.

It was terrifying! No attic floor could stand the impact. Panic-stricken, he jumped out of bed. Instantly there was an uncanny silence. He went shakily to the bathroom, trying to persuade himself it had been a dreadful nightmare. Cautiously he climbed back into bed — and instantly the thunderous noise started up again!

He shot out of bed and scurried into his wife's room — head cold or no head cold — hugging her tight for warmth and comfort.

'Been dreaming?' she slurred, and was asleep again.

Next morning, he went out on to the landing. To his horror it was strewn with books and two chair seats. In one of the other rooms an old Teddy Bear had been stuffed head-first into the waste paper basket.

In the spare room where he had started the night his son's theses papers had been placed on the floor, still in order and each of the three chairs they had been on was wet.

'You've not made it to the bathroom!' was his wife's sceptic comment.

※※※

Several months later, the previous owners of the house, who were friends of theirs, were invited to tea. The husband noticed they had made some alterations and was given a guided tour. As they passed the open door of the spare room and seeing it furnished he said with a wry smile, 'So you've cured the water problem?'

***

In 1883 THE CROWN HOTEL in Market Street experienced a piano playing phantom in a room that contained no piano, the sound of two panic-stricken children plus NOISES IN THE ATTIC OF CLUMPING FEET AND THE MOVING OF GREAT CHESTS!

***

And now my 'co-incidence factor' made itself known again. I was looking for something quite different in my research papers and came across some Court Documents of 1639 relating to the theft of five barrels of gunpowder. A certain William Fox said upon his oath that he had been at William Padner's house in Poole until about ten of the clock. On departing he met with Clement Short, a mariner and went with him to his house. He stayed a while, talking of Newfoundland and sea matters until about 1 of the clock. On the way to his lodgings he heard whispering, rummaging and a TUMBLING NOISE IN ONE OF THE ATTICS at 'Browne's little lane'. (Unfortunately this name does not now exist. Did it lead into Market Street?) There were two long barrels, three bigger ones and four smaller ones stored in Paradise Cellars containing various substances described as 'soap, mustard seed and gunpowder'. Could the guilty parties of long ago still be trying to move their ill-gotten wares?

***

Also in Market Street is the lovely Guildhall building, until recently a museum. Previously the ground floor was used as a market while the upper floor was a large council chamber with a smaller chamber at the north east end. Above these chambers are small rooms reached by a narrow staircase. Museum attendants alone in the buildings have described hearing footsteps believed to be those of a former accountant, Mr Jubber, who committed suicide by hanging himself there in the 19th century.

***

Byngley House in Market Street has a weird, suffocating atmosphere in one of the bedrooms but as far as I know, no apparitions.

When the house was open to the public I was asked by its owner to transcribe from Tudor script into readable English the Last Will and Testament of Thomas White who owned it in 1555.

He had been mayor on several occasions and was a very wealthy man, having shares in at least 16 manors in the surrounding countryside as well as 'household stuffe' and other riches. He was a Papist and 'put up an altar' in his house when he was not allowed to preach in the parish church but when his manservant put his hand out of the window to ring the bell for Mass he was threatened by Reformers that a hand-gun would make him smart if he did so!

Market Street is certainly full of history!

The Boy in White, Coy Pond's ghost, Branksome

Some years ago, a lady was walking her dog at the pretty little park called Coy Pond when she met a youth in a white macintosh. He smiled at her — and disappeared into thin air!

Mrs Bedford told me that it was believed to have been the ghost of a boy who murdered a council workman at that spot. She had worked with the boy's mother at one of Bournemouth's top hotels and it was she who had told her the full story.

The boy, who used to act strangely at times set out from Bournemouth Gardens near the Pier wearing his white raincoat and walked through the length of the Gardens — about 2 miles — until he reached Coy Pond. He had been having one of his strange turns that day, unfortunately for the victim who was cutting grass. Without any warning, the boy seized the man's scythe and hacked him to death. Leaving the body where it had fallen he went home, hiding his bloodstained raincoat behind a boiler where his mother eventually found it and told the police.

The boy was tried and convicted but was only sentenced to three years imprisonment as his mind was disturbed.

After three years he was released, but only lived for a few more years. One day when driving through the New Forest, he stopped at a garage for petrol at Lyndhurst and died at the petrol pump. His parents too are now dead — but the Boy in White's spirit returns to the scene of the crime ...

The Strange Spoon

Since I began writing this book, I have been 'visited' by a spoon! I was about to make a cup of coffee, and there it was inside the jar which was half full, as I had been using it for a couple of weeks. I could not have spooned coffee out without seeing it and as I was living alone at the time no-one could have put it there.

My sister had called the day before and finding I was out, she and her husband let themselves in with their key and made themselves cups of coffee. The next time I saw her I said jokingly, 'You didn't have to bring your own spoon, you know!' and explained how I had found it in the jar. She told me it was in the jar when she opened it! But it most certainly had not been there the day before!

Carefully, I examined the jar. There was no mention of a free offer so I put the spoon back to see if it could be hidden by the coffee but that was impossible. It was transparent, like nothing I own and rather too small in the bowl for a measure of coffee, shaped rather like a larger than usual mustard spoon — very prosaic!

I still have it. It hasn't de-materialised or anything, but I would love to know where it came from!